WOMEN OF THE CIVIL WAR THROUGH PRIMARY SOURCES

Carin T. Ford

Enslow Publishers, Inc.
40 Industrial Road
Box 398
Berkeley Heights, NJ 07922
USA

http://www.enslow.com

Original edition published as *Daring Women of the Civil War* in 2004.

Library of Congress Cataloging-in-Publication Data

Ford, Carin T.

   Women of the Civil War through primary sources / Carin T. Ford.
     p. cm. — (The Civil War through primary sources)
   "Original edition published as Daring Women of the Civil War in 2004."
   Includes bibliographical references and index.
   Summary: "Explores the lives and roles of women during the Civil War, including their work as nurses, spies, and soldiers, as well as daily life and work on the home front"—Provided by publisher.
   ISBN 978-0-7660-4128-8
   1. United States—History—Civil War, 1861–1865—Women—Juvenile literature. 2. United States—History—Civil War, 1861–1865—Participation, Female—Juvenile literature. 3. United States—History—Civil War, 1861–1865—Social aspects—Juvenile literature. I. Ford, Carin T. Daring women of the Civil War. II. Title.
   E628.F67 2014
   973.7082—dc23
               2012036350

Future editions:
Paperback ISBN: 978-1-4644-0186-2
EPUB ISBN: 978-1-4645-1099-1
Single-User PDF ISBN: 978-1-4646-1099-8
Multi-User PDF ISBN: 978-0-7660-5728-9

Printed in the United States of America
012013 The HF Group, North Manchester, IN

10 9 8 7 6 5 4 3 2 1

To Our Readers: We have done our best to make sure all Internet addresses in this book were active and appropriate when we went to press. However, the author and the publisher have no control over and assume no liability for the material available on those Internet sites or on other Web sites they may link to. Any comments or suggestions can be sent by e-mail to comments@enslow.com or to the address on the back cover.

Illustration Credits: *A Diary From Dixie, as Written by Mary Boykin Chesnut, Wife of James Chesnut, Jr., United States Senator From South Carolina, 1859–1861, and Afterward an Aide to Jefferson Davis and a Brigadier-General in the Confederate Army,* © 1905, frontispiece, page xii, p. 13; Gettysburg National Military Park, p. 15; The Granger Collection, NYC, pp. 33, 36; Library of Congress Prints and Photographs, pp. 1, 2, 3, 4, 5, 9, 12, 16, 19, 20, 24, 28, 29, 35, 38, 39, 40; Library of Congress Rare Books and Manuscripts Division, p. 10; Used by permission of Louisa May Alcott's Orchard House, p. 7; National Archives and Records Administration, pp. 21, 26, 31; U.S. Army, p. 27.

Cover Illustration: The Granger Collection, NYC (Illustration of Clara Barton aiding a wounded soldier in the Civil War).

CONTENTS

─────★─────

LOOK FOR THIS SYMBOL **PRIMARY SOURCE** TO FIND THE PRIMARY SOURCES THROUGHOUT THIS BOOK.

In this Civil War-era photograph, two unidentified women read letters from their loved ones. Many women, including Louisa May Alcott, wrote diaries and letters during the Civil War.

CHAPTER 1

★

WOMEN'S WORK

It was April 1861, and Louisa May Alcott wrote in her diary, "I long to be a man."[1]

The Civil War had just begun. Alcott was twenty-nine years old and wanted to be a soldier.

But Alcott could not join the army. She was a woman—and "women's work" was in the house. Their jobs were cooking, cleaning, sewing, washing, and caring for children. Women's work did not include being a soldier.

There were many things that the laws of the United States did not allow women to do in the 1800s:

- They could not vote.

- They could not own property.

- They could not serve on juries.

- They could not be elected to political office.

When the Civil War broke out, men had to leave their homes and jobs to become soldiers. Women suddenly found themselves taking on new roles and more responsibilities than they ever had before.

Why was the United States being torn apart by war? The bad feelings between the North and South had started with slavery. Most Southerners were farmers, and their biggest crop was cotton. To produce millions of bales of cotton each year, the farmers needed plenty of field workers.

Their answer was African slaves—people who were kidnapped in Africa and brought to America in chains. Slaves did not have to be paid. They were property, bought and sold like animals. The owners forced their slaves to work.

Louisa May Alcott (1832–1888)

Louisa May Alcott was born in Germantown, Pennsylvania. She began writing at an early age and had some poetry and short stories published in popular magazines. In 1854, she wrote her first book, *Flower Fables*.

As a nurse in the Civil War, Alcott came down with typhoid fever after only six weeks on the job. She was sent home. She based the book *Hospital Sketches* (published in 1863) on her time as a nurse.

When Alcott was in her mid-thirties, her publisher asked her to write a book for girls. The result was her most famous work, *Little Women*, a novel set in New England during the Civil War. Louisa went on to write more than thirty books.

Louisa May Alcott

PRIMARY
SOURCE

The businesses, factories, and small farms in the North did not need slaves. Also, most Northerners believed it was wrong for one person to own another. One by one, the states in the North put an end to slavery. Yet some Northerners wanted to see slavery stopped in the South, too.

When women first joined the struggle against slavery, they used the only weapon they had: their words.

Angelina Grimké grew up in Charleston, South Carolina. Her family owned many slaves. As a teenager, Angelina saw a young slave whose master had whipped him so badly that the boy could hardly walk. Angelina knew this was not right.

When she was older, Grimké and her sister, Sarah, left their home and headed North. There, the two women wrote newspaper articles and gave speeches against slavery. However, most Northerners did not care about slaves in the South, and they thought speaking in public was not ladylike. Crowds often made fun of the sisters and threw apples at them.[2]

One of the strongest voices against slavery was a runaway slave who called herself Sojourner Truth. She used her loud voice and sharp wit as weapons against slavery. Often, her audiences

After escaping slavery, Sojourner Truth, pictured here in 1864, toured parts of the country, speaking out against slavery.

PRIMARY SOURCE

cried as she talked about the horrors that she and other slaves had suffered.

The woman with the most powerful words of all was Harriet Beecher Stowe. In 1851, Stowe started writing *Uncle Tom's Cabin*, about an old slave named Uncle Tom and his cruel master, Simon Legree. Reading this heartbreaking story made many Northerners more upset and angry about slavery than ever before.[3]

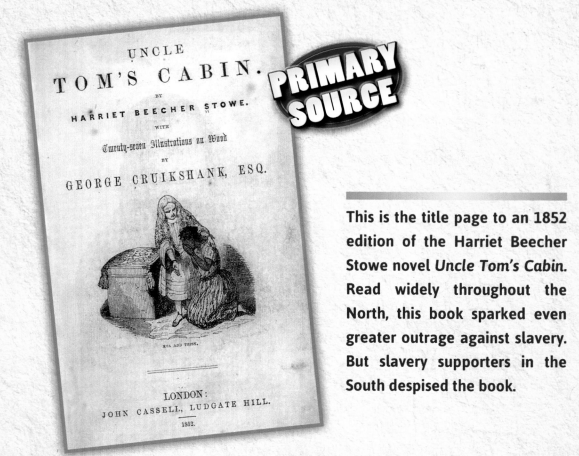

This is the title page to an 1852 edition of the Harriet Beecher Stowe novel *Uncle Tom's Cabin*. Read widely throughout the North, this book sparked even greater outrage against slavery. But slavery supporters in the South despised the book.

Seceding From the Union

★ Secede means "to break away." Eleven Southern states seceded from the United States.

★ President Abraham Lincoln began fighting the Civil War because he did not want the nation split in two.

When Abraham Lincoln was elected president in 1860, many Southerners were afraid he would put an end to slavery. Seven Southern states—South Carolina, Alabama, Florida, Mississippi, Louisiana, Texas, and Georgia—broke away from the United States. They formed their own country, the Confederate States of America. Lincoln wanted to keep the country united, and fighting broke out between the North and South. Soon, Virginia, Arkansas, Tennessee, and North Carolina joined the Confederacy.

Few people thought the Civil War would last long. But as the fighting dragged on for four bloody years, it became clear that more help was needed, both at home and on the battlefield.

CHAPTER 2

★

THE HOME FRONT

"They are coming! The Yankees are coming at last!" wrote Sarah Morgan Dawson in her diary on March 14, 1863. Union troops were pushing their way toward her home in Louisiana. "For four or five hours the sound of their cannon has assailed our ears. There!—that one shook my bed!"[1]

Like countless other women in the North and South, Dawson kept a diary during the Civil War. For some women, writing helped pass the time. For nearly all, it was a way to express worries, hopes, and fears.

Mary Boykin Chesnut wrote the most famous diary of the war years. She filled fifty notebooks with more than 400,000 words.

Florida

Yesterday on the tra...
...before we reached Fern...
"dina" a woman cried out...
="That settles the hash".
Fanny touched me on the sho...
—"Look out! Lincoln' ele...
"How do you know?"—
"The man over there has a...
The excitement was b...
Everybody was talking a...
same time. One, a li...
moved than the others I
saying despontly— "the
die is Cast— No more vain
regrets— Sad forebodings are
useless. The stake is life or
death—"
"Now did you ever!" was
the prevailing exclamation.

This is a reproduction of a page from Mary Boykin Chesnut's diary. The portrait of Chesnut (right) is from the frontispiece to her published diary.

Chesnut was a wealthy Southerner whose family owned many slaves. She described the events of the war in great detail.

"At half-past four the heavy booming of a cannon," she wrote when the Confederate soldiers fired on Fort Sumter. "I sprang out of bed and on my knees. . . . I prayed as I never prayed before."[2]

In the North, many of the women who kept diaries wrote about being wartime nurses and working to end slavery. Sophronia Bucklin described nursing the soldiers at a war hospital set up near the battlefield. Her diary was published as *In Hospital and Camp*. Laura Haviland of Michigan wrote *A Woman's Life-Work*.

Who's Who in the Civil War

★ The North was also known as the Union, or the United States. The people there were often called Yankees.

★ The South was called the Confederacy, or the Confederate States. During the war, Southerners were sometimes called Rebels, or Johnny Reb.

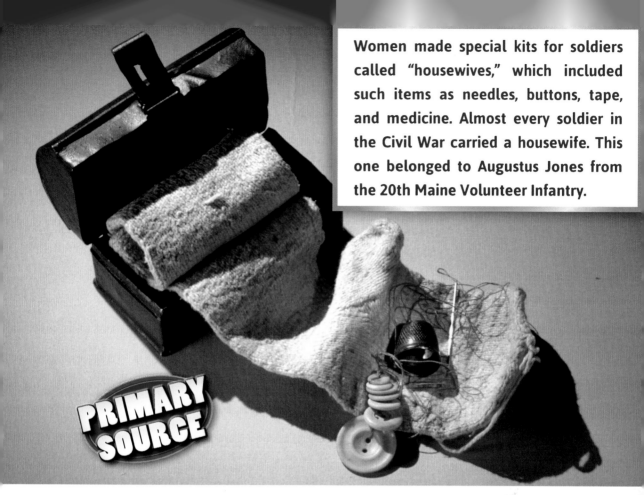

Women made special kits for soldiers called "housewives," which included such items as needles, buttons, tape, and medicine. Almost every soldier in the Civil War carried a housewife. This one belonged to Augustus Jones from the 20th Maine Volunteer Infantry.

PRIMARY SOURCE

She told of her work on the Underground Railroad. This secret network of people and escape routes helped thousands of slaves run away to freedom. Twelve-year-old Tillie Pierce Alleman wrote about seeing the Battle of Gettysburg in *At Gettysburg or What a Girl Saw and Heard of the Battle.*

Most women could not sit still during the war.

"Their cause is our cause," said one Georgia woman. "We can work for those who go and [we can] pray. . . ."[3]

Many women joined soldiers' aid societies. These groups sewed soldiers' uniforms, hospital clothing, and bandages.

Women also put together small bags called comforts or hussies, which stood for "housewives."[4] They filled these bags for the soldiers with pins, needles, buttons, tape, quinine (a medicine), and other small goods.

Most battles of the Civil War were fought in the South. So the war had an even greater effect on the lives of Southern women.

PRIMARY SOURCE

Many women joined soldiers' aid societies to make supplies and care for the soldiers. In this April 1865 photo, a group of women stands outside the United States Christian Commission building, one such soldiers' aid society created during the war.

Union Soldiers in the South

★ As the Union soldiers swept through the South, they destroyed everything they did not need. They did not want to leave anything behind that the Confederate army could use.

★ Many Southern women saw their slaves set free, their homes burned, and their animals killed.

Their husbands, brothers, and sons had joined the Confederate army. Southern women had no choice but to take charge of their households.

In the towns, small farms, and large plantations of the South, women prepared food and cared for their children. But now they had to do the men's work, too. They planted crops, plowed fields, cut firewood, and fed the animals. For many, this was the first time in their lives that they had ever worked so hard. "I find myself, every day, doing something I never did before," wrote Mary Lee of Virginia.[5]

Their work was made even more difficult by the North's wartime plan. Northern ships blocked Southern ports, so ships could not deliver their cargo of food, clothing, and other goods. The women of the South had to make shoes out of cloth or paper, twist rags into candles, and use berry juice as ink for their pens.

Women also spun thread on spinning wheels, then wove it into cloth on their looms. Many took up knitting and sewing. They cut up their dresses to make flags and men's shirts. They trimmed their carpets into blankets. Countless hours were spent knitting mittens and socks for the soldiers. One South Carolina woman said, "We spent all our spare time knitting socks . . . and we never went out to pay a visit without taking our knitting along."[6]

In addition, businesses needed workers to replace the men off at war. Large numbers of women took jobs in offices. Others were hired by factories that made weapons and war goods. From 1860 to 1870, the number of women earning salaries more than doubled.[7]

CHAPTER 3

⭐

SERVING AS NURSES

As soon as the Civil War began, hundreds of women on both sides wanted to be nurses in hospitals. They were quickly given the same answer: "It is no place for women."[1]

At that time, army hospitals had male nurses. Most were patients who had gotten better. These soldiers were often still weak from their wounds or illness—but at least they were men. In those days, it was simply not considered proper for a woman to take care of a male stranger. Also, people thought women were too delicate for the shocking sights of death, disease, and crippled bodies.

As the war went on, the number of wounded soldiers continued to grow. More help was desperately needed in the hospitals.

Dorothea "Dragon" Dix hired and trained the nurses for the Union army.

At last, women were allowed to take part. Dorothea Dix was given the job of hiring and training nurses for the Union army. Nicknamed "Dragon Dix," she had spent more than twenty years working in mental hospitals and prisons.

Dix wanted to be sure that her female nurses were taken seriously. She hired only plain-looking women who were older than thirty. The nurses had to dress in brown or black. They could not wear bows, curls, jewelry, or fancy skirts.[2] Although Dix was strict, at least two thousand women went to work for her.

Many people in the hospitals still did not think women should be nurses. Georgeanna M. Woolsey, one of the first nurses to work in a Union army hospital, wrote, "Hardly a surgeon of whom I can think, received or treated [nurses] with even common courtesy."[3]

Like male nurses, most women had no training for the job. Still, they were able to help in a number of ways. "Till noon I trot, trot giving out rations, cutting up food for helpless 'boys,' washing faces . . . dressing wounds . . . dusting tables, sewing bandages, keeping my tray tidy, rushing up & down with pillows, bed linen,

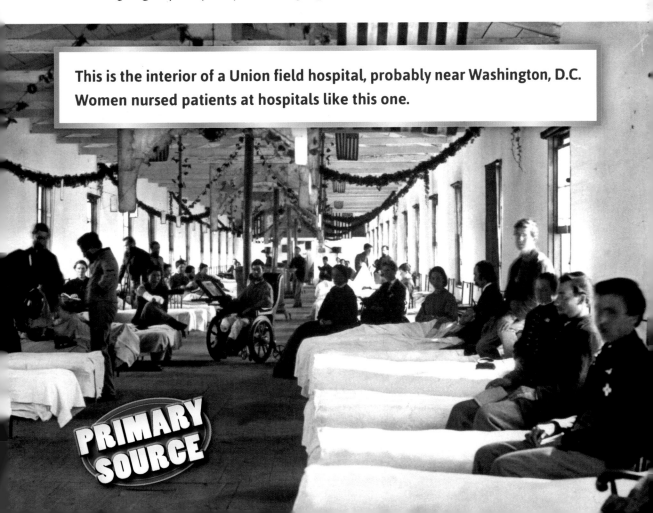

This is the interior of a Union field hospital, probably near Washington, D.C. Women nursed patients at hospitals like this one.

PRIMARY SOURCE

The U.S. Sanitary Commission

The Sanitary Commission was founded in June 1861. Its goal was to take care of the soldiers' health by keeping the camps and hospitals clean (sanitary). With the help of hundreds of women, the Sanitary Commission collected food, clothing, and medical supplies for the soldiers. Workers also held bake sales and carnivals, called sanitary fairs. They raised millions of dollars for the war.

"God knows what we should have done without them," said Frederick Law Olmsted, secretary of the commission. "They have worked like heroes night and day."[4]

sponges, books & directions, till it seems as if I would joyfully [give anything] for fifteen minutes rest," wrote Louisa May Alcott.[5] She was helping out in a Union hospital in Washington, D.C.

Nurses were not given much to eat, and they often worked all night long with no rest. Sometimes the only place they could sleep was on the floor, their clothing splattered with blood from the wounded soldiers.

In the hospitals set up near battlefields, the job was even harder. Nurses could be called to work at any time of the day or night. They were tired all the time and often slept on the cold ground. Their hands swelled, and their feet blistered. They could be killed by nearby gunfire.

Still, the work went on.

Clara Barton was known as the "Angel of the Battlefield."[6] At the start of the war, she worked in a government office in Washington, D.C. When she learned that hundreds of wounded soldiers needed medical supplies, Barton jumped into action. She put ads in newspapers to gather what was needed. Then she came up with a plan to bring the supplies to the soldiers.

Traveling into the war area with mules and wagons, Barton said, "I went in while the battle raged."[7] She would later go on to set up the American Red Cross. Today, this organization continues to help sick and wounded people during wars, floods, and other disasters.

Mary Ann "Mother" Bickerdyke traveled to nineteen battlefields during the four years of the Civil War. She cleaned

Clara Barton

hospital buildings for the Union army and ordered bathtubs to be made from barrels. She set up kitchens to make sure the soldiers ate healthy foods. If she saw dishonest or lazy workers, she had them fired from their jobs. Often she walked about the battlefields at night with a lantern, searching for wounded soldiers.

Susie King Taylor was a runaway slave from Georgia. During the Civil War, she worked as a laundress and nurse in an African-American regiment of the Union army. Taylor also taught the soldiers to read and write. She had learned these skills from her master's daughter.[8]

In the South, most hospitals would not allow women to care for wounded soldiers. Yet many Confederate women simply took matters into their own hands. During the first Battle of Bull Run, women from Virginia came to the battlefield and took care of injured soldiers throughout the day and night.[9]

In cities, such as Atlanta, Georgia, and Chattanooga, Tennessee, private homes were set up to offer food, shelter, and rest to sick soldiers.[10]

Sally Tomkins used her own money to turn her friend's Richmond, Virginia, home into a hospital. There, Tomkins cared for more than a thousand wounded soldiers. She was the only woman to be made an officer in the Confederate army.

Juliet Opie Hopkins also spent her money and time in Richmond hospitals. She took charge of caring for wounded soldiers from Alabama. In thanks for her work, Alabama lawmakers printed Hopkins's picture on its state money.

Kate Cumming, also of Alabama, helped nurse Confederate soldiers in a Mississippi hotel that was turned into a hospital. In April 1862, Cumming wrote in her diary that wounded soldiers

Dr. Mary Edwards Walker

Very few women in the United States were doctors in the mid-1800s. Dr. Mary Edwards Walker wanted to be a surgeon for the Union army, but she was turned down. Walker did not give up. Wearing pants, suspenders, and a knee-length dress, she volunteered her skills in a hospital in Washington, D.C. Walker wrote that her patients were "very much pleased" to see her—even if the male doctors were not.[11] Near the end of the war, Walker was finally hired as an army surgeon. She was the only woman in the war to be awarded the Congressional Medal of Honor. This is the highest honor given to a citizen of the United States.

Mary Edwards Walker, pictured here wearing the Congressional Medal of Honor, was the only woman to receive the award during the Civil War.

PRIMARY SOURCE

were lying "so close together that it was almost impossible to walk without stepping on them. . . . I sat up all night, bathing the men's wounds, and giving them water."[12]

The work was difficult, but the women did not give up. They kept the hospitals clean and organized, and they took good care of the soldiers. In addition, women cheered up their patients by singing in the wards, writing letters for the soldiers, and hanging bright curtains from the hospital windows.[13]

The work of these female nurses made a big difference. One study of hospitals reported that the patients were better off when female nurses cared for them. Twice as many patients died under the care of male nurses.[14]

Susie King Taylor was one of the first African-American nurses.

PRIMARY SOURCE

CHAPTER 4

FIGHTING AS SOLDIERS

In the spring of 1864, Private Lyons Wakeman fell ill and was sent to a hospital in New Orleans, Louisiana. About six weeks later, the soldier died. There was nothing unusual about Wakeman's death. For every soldier killed in battle during the war, two others died from disease.[1]

But Private Wakeman was different from the other soldiers. "He" was a woman.

At least four hundred women disguised themselves as men and fought in the Civil War. Some women joined the army because they did not want to be parted from their husbands. Some wanted to serve their country. Others were just looking for adventure.

Frances Clalin Clayton disguised herself as a man, "Jack Williams," to join the Union army. Serving in Missouri artillery and cavalry units, she was wounded in the battles of Shiloh and Stone River. In 1865, Clayton posed for these photos, one in full uniform and one in a dress, after completing her service.

Nineteen-year-old Sarah Rosetta Wakeman was tired of staying home on the family farm. So she gave her name as "Lyons," claimed she was twenty-one, and joined the army.

"I [am] enjoying my Self better this summer than I ever did before in this world," she wrote to her family in June 1863. "I have good Clothing and enough to eat and nothing to do, only to handle my gun and that I can do as well as the rest of them."[2]

Women were not allowed to become soldiers, so they had to pretend to be men. They wore men's clothing, cut their hair short, and used men's names.

Loreta Janeta Velazquez had been interested in war since she was a child. In the Civil War, she fought for the Confederacy under the name Harry Buford. "Braiding my hair very close, I put on a man's wig, and a false mustache, and by tucking my pantaloons in my boots . . . I managed to transform myself into a very presentable man," she wrote.[3]

Female soldiers not only needed to look like men, but they also needed to *act* like men, too. They learned to drink, smoke, and chew tobacco, like the other soldiers. When they were wounded,

Following the Troops

Not all women who followed the troops served as nurses or soldiers. Some were soldiers' wives, girlfriends, or relatives as well as laundresses.

Vivandières (which means "hospitality givers") and the Daughters of the Regiment also traveled with the soldiers. They took part in parades and drills and often got a taste of battle. They carried water for the wounded soldiers, did laundry, and waved the company flag. These women usually wore sashes and lively uniforms. August Foster was a Daughter of the Regiment with the Second Maine Infantry. She spent most of her time nursing wounded soldiers. At Bull Run, she had her horse shot out from under her.

Vivandières traveled with the soldiers, taking part in drills and parades as well as carrying water to wounded soldiers. This portrait shows Mary Tippee, a *Vivandière* with the Collis Zouaves.

female soldiers often refused medical care. They did not want to take off their clothing.

In 1863, one Indiana cavalryman wrote: "We discovered last week a soldier who turned out to be a girl. She had already been in service for twenty-one months and was twice wounded. Maybe she would have remained undiscovered for a long time if she hadn't fainted. She was given a warm bath which gave the secret away."[4]

Keeping Their Secrets

★ In daily army life, undressing was not usually a problem for women. Soldiers were always on the move. They could go for weeks without changing their clothes. For bathing, soldiers had time to wash only their faces and hands.

★ Many women would move to another unit if they were in danger of being found out. Elizabeth Compton spent eighteen months in seven different units. Frances Hook served in units in Illinois, Michigan, and Tennessee.

PRIMARY SOURCE

Jennie Hodgers, pictured here in 1864, disguised herself as a man and used the name Albert Cashier in order to serve as a soldier in the Union army's 95th Illinois Regiment.

Amy Clarke used the name Richard Anderson to join a Tennessee unit of the Confederacy. Fighting alongside her husband, she buried him on the battlefield at Shiloh. But Clarke continued fighting until she was wounded in her ankle and chest. She was captured by Union soldiers and sent back to the Confederates—in a dress.

Jennie Hodgers joined the Union army in Illinois in 1862. The nineteen-year-old called herself Albert Cashier and fought in several battles, including the Battle of Vicksburg. After serving three years in the war, Hodgers kept up the disguise. Her true identity was discovered in 1911, when she broke her leg in a car accident. A doctor discovered that his patient was a woman, but he agreed to keep her secret.

Soldiers stood guard in all weather, marched for countless miles, and fought on the battlefield. A soldier's life was not easy. But for several hundred women—most of whose names will never even be known—the decision to join the army was the right one.

"The weather is cold and the ground is froze hard, but I sleep as warm in the tents as I would in a good bed," wrote Wakeman in December 1862. "I like to be a soldier very well."[5]

CHAPTER 5

BECOMING SPIES

A group of slaves was building a fort for the Confederate army. They were using pickaxes, shovels, and wheelbarrows. The work was hot and sweaty. Suddenly, one slave pointed at another, saying that the man seemed to be "turning white."[1]

The "slave" who was turning white was really Sarah Emma Edmonds. She had fought for the Union under the name Frank Thompson. Now she was a spy. Wearing a dark wool wig, Edmonds was a white woman whose black makeup was fading as she sweated in the hot sun.

Edmonds worked among the Confederate soldiers and listened to their battle plans. When night came, she slipped away

PRIMARY SOURCE

Elizabeth Van Lew, a Union army spy, carried this cipher code in her watch case until her death in 1900.

to deliver the information to the Union army. She was one of dozens of women in the North and South who risked their lives to spy on the enemy.

Mary Elizabeth Bowser was an ex-slave who spied for the Union. She worked for her former owner, Elizabeth Van Lew, who was known as "Crazy Bet."[2] She purposely acted odd so people would not suspect her of running a spy ring.

Bowser worked as a servant in the home of Jefferson Davis. He was the president of the Confederate States. Bowser listened closely to Davis's conversations with his dinner guests. She also looked at telegrams and important papers lying around the house. Everyone thought Bowser could not read, so these papers were not hidden away.

Each night, Bowser returned home to tell Van Lew what she had learned. Van Lew wrote everything down and hid the papers in the soles of boots or inside eggshells. Sometimes her notes were baked into loaves of bread. Then the hidden messages were delivered to the Union army.

Like Bowser, Harriet Tubman was a former slave who spied for the Union. Through the years, she led more than three hundred slaves to freedom on the Underground Railroad.[3] Because she knew the countryside well, Tubman searched for Confederate camps during the war. She told Union soldiers about the enemy's location. In 1863, she went on a gunboat raid in South Carolina with Colonel James Montgomery and his troops. With information she had gathered, Tubman helped the Union

Being a Smuggler

Some women smuggled important goods, such as guns and medicine, across enemy lines. They would often hide pistols and the medicine quinine in the false bottoms of trunks as well as in their parasols and big hoop skirts.

After guiding many slaves to freedom on the Underground Railroad, Harriet Tubman served as a spy for the Union.

PRIMARY SOURCE

soldiers make a surprise attack on the Confederates.[4]

Actress Pauline Cushman did shows for Confederate troops. Whenever she heard soldiers talking about war plans, she secretly sent the information to Union officers. When Cushman was caught, she was sentenced to death. But the Union army captured the town, and Cushman was freed. She returned to acting after the war.

Belle Boyd of West Virginia worked for the Confederacy. A young woman with a great deal of charm, Boyd made friends with Union soldiers. Then she passed along information about battle plans to the Confederate generals. One time, Union officers were meeting at a room in her aunt's home. Boyd knew about a closet upstairs with a hole in the floor. Boyd wrote, "I stole softly upstairs, and, lying on the floor of the closet, applied my ear to the hole, and found, to my great joy, I could distinctly hear the conversation that was passing below."[5]

Boyd wrote the information in code and brought it to the Confederate army. After the war, Boyd went onstage, doing shows about her life as a spy.

A rich widow in her forties, Rose O'Neal Greenhow gave many parties for important people in Washington, D.C. She was also a Confederate spy. In talking to Union army officers, she learned how many soldiers, and which roads, the Union planned to use in their attack on Manassas, Virginia, in 1861. She sent a coded message with her friend, who was disguised as a farm girl. Greenhow's friend carried the

Belle Boyd was a very successful Confederate spy.

PRIMARY SOURCE

note in a bun in her hair. Some historians give Greenhow partial credit for the Confederate victory at the first Battle of Bull Run.

Although many female spies were caught and put in prison, some worked throughout the war without being discovered. Yet all were willing to give their lives for what they believed in. Written on the grave of Elizabeth Van Lew are the words: "She risked everything that is dear to man—friends, fortune, comfort, health, life itself."[6]

Although women had proven that they could easily handle "men's work" during the Civil War, it would be a long time before they achieved equal rights. It would take more than fifty years after the war ended before women gained the right to vote. In this 1917 photo, a women's suffrage group pickets outside the White House.

Voting Rights

★ African-American men were given the right to vote in 1870 with the Fifteenth Amendment to the Constitution.

★ Women—both black and white—could not vote until fifty years later, in 1920, when the Nineteenth Amendment was passed.

After the Civil War ended, many women wanted to continue in the new roles they had taken on during the past four years. But the husbands, brothers, and sons who returned home took charge once again. Women went back to the work they had done before the war.

Still, everything was not the same. Women had proved that they were very capable of doing "men's work." Over time, their voices would grow louder and stronger in demanding to be treated equally.

TIMELINE

Pre-1860s

1835: Angelina Grimké joins the abolitionist movement.

1843: Isabella Baumfree changes her name to Sojourner Truth and begins speaking out against slavery.

1850: Harriet Tubman makes the first of many trips south on the Underground Railroad.

1851: Harriet Beecher Stowe's *Uncle Tom's Cabin* appears in newspapers as a weekly series.

1860

November 6: Abraham Lincoln is elected president of the United States.

December 20: South Carolina secedes from the United States.

1861

February: Six more Southern states secede, and the Confederate States of America is formed, with Jefferson Davis as president.

April 12: Shots are fired at Fort Sumter, and the Civil War begins.

April–June: Four more Southern states secede.

June 18: The United States Sanitary Commission is set up to provide care for wounded soldiers.

July: Rose O'Neal Greenhow's spying helps the Confederates win the first Battle of Bull Run.

Dorothea Dix is put in charge of all women nurses working in Union hospitals.

Clara Barton brings supplies to the Union army.

Harriet Tubman begins spying for the Union army.

1862

Susie King Taylor begins as a laundress and then becomes a nurse for the Union.

1863

January 1: Lincoln issues the Emancipation Proclamation.

May–June: Louisa May Alcott publishes *Hospital Sketches*, which tells of her experiences as a war nurse in Washington, D.C.

June: Harriet Tubman assists Colonel James Montgomery as a scout on a gunboat raid in South Carolina.

July 3: The Union wins the Battle of Gettysburg.

November 19: President Lincoln gives the Gettysburg Address.

1864

March: Ulysses S. Grant is named commander of the Union army.

November 8: Lincoln is elected to a second term as president.

1865

April 9: Confederate general Robert E. Lee surrenders to Union general Ulysses S. Grant.

April 14: President Lincoln is assassinated.

April 15: Andrew Johnson becomes president.

November 11: Dr. Mary Edwards Walker receives the Congressional Medal of Honor.

December 6: The Thirteenth Amendment to the Constitution abolishes slavery in the United States.

CHAPTER NOTES

CHAPTER 1. WOMEN'S WORK

1. Joel Myerson and Daniel Shealy, eds., *The Journals of Louisa May Alcott* (Boston: Little, Brown, and Company, 1989), p. 105.
2. "The Legendary Ladies of the Civil War," *Civil War Women . . . They Ain't No Scarlett O'Hara*, 2001, <http://www.civilwarwomen.homestead.com> (June 12, 2003).
3. Geoffrey C. Ward, *The Civil War: An Illustrated History* (New York: Knopf, 1990), p. 19.

CHAPTER 2. THE HOME FRONT

1. Sarah Morgan Dawson, *A Confederate Girl's Diary* (Athens, Ga.: University of Georgia Press, 1991), p. 438.
2. Mary Boykin Chesnut, *A Diary From Dixie* (Chapel Hill, N.C.: University of North Carolina Press, 1997), p. 35.
3. William C. Davis, *Look Away! A History of the Confederate States of America* (New York: The Free Press, 2002), p. 194.
4. Agatha Young, *Women and the Crisis: Women of the North in the Civil War* (New York: McDowell, Obolensky, 1959), p. 69.
5. Drew Gilpin Faust, *Mothers of Invention: Women of the Slaveholding South in the Civil War* (Chapel Hill, N.C.: The University of North Carolina Press, 1996), p. 49.
6. Bell Irvin Wiley, *Confederate Women* (New York: Barnes and Noble Books, 1975), p. 145.
7. Mary Elizabeth Massey, *Bonnet Brigades* (New York: Alfred A. Knopf, 1966), p. 151.

CHAPTER 3. SERVING AS NURSES

1. Sylvia Dannett, *Noble Women of the North* (New York: T. Yoseloff, 1959), p. 68.
2. Agatha Young, *The Women and the Crisis* (New York: McDowell, Obolensky, 1959), p. 98.
3. Mary P. Ryan, *Womanhood in America: From Colonial Times to the Present* (New York: New Viewpoints, 1975; new edition, 1983), p. 200.
4. Mary Elizabeth Massey, *Bonnet Brigades* (New York: Alfred A. Knopf, 1966), p. 54.
5. Joel Myerson and Daniel Shealy, eds., *The Journals of Louisa May Alcott* (Boston: Little, Brown, and Company, 1989), p. 114.
6. Life Stories of Civil War Heroes, 2001–2003, <http://www.geocities.com/Athens/Aegean/6732/cb.html> (June 12, 2003).
7. "Civil War Nurses, Angels of the Battlefield," *Shotgun's Home of the American Civil War,* n.d., <http://www.civilwarhome.com/civilwarnurses.htm> (June 12, 2003).

8. Charles H. Wesley and Patricia W. Romero, *Negro Americans in the Civil War: From Slavery to Citizenship* (New York: Publishers Company, Inc., 1967), p. 108.

9. William C. Davis, *Look Away! A History of the Confederate States of America* (New York: Free Press, 2002), p. 195.

10. Bell Irvin Wiley, *Confederate Women* (New York: Barnes and Noble Books, 1975), p. 144.

11. Elizabeth D. Leonard, *Yankee Women: Gender Battles in the Civil War* (New York: W. W. Norton & Company, 1994), p. 117.

12. Katharine M. Jones, *Heroines of Dixie* (New York: Konecky & Konecky, 1955), p. 109.

13. George Worthington Adams, *Doctors in Blue: The Medical History of the Union Army in the Civil War* (Baton Rouge, La.: Louisiana State University Press, 1952), p. 163.

14. Drew Gilpin Faust, *Mothers of Invention: Women of the Slaveholding South in the Civil War* (Chapel Hill: The University of North Carolina Press, 1996), p. 97.

CHAPTER 4. FIGHTING AS SOLDIERS

1. Shelby Foote, *The Civil War: A Narrative, Red River to Appomattox* (New York: Random House, 1974), vol. 3, p. 1,040.

2. Lauren Cook Burgess, *An Uncommon Soldier* (Pasadena, Md.: The Minerva Center, 1994), p. 31.

3. Loreta Janeta Velazquez, *The Woman in Battle: A Narrative of the Exploits, Adventures, and Travels of Madame Loreta Janeta Velaquez* (Richondz: Dustin, Gilman & Co., 1876), p. 53.

4. Wendy A. King, *Clad in Uniform: Women Soldiers of the Civil War*, n.d., <http://www.geocities.com/womansoldier/womenofficers. html> (June 12, 2003).

5. Burgess, pp. 21–22.

CHAPTER 5. BECOMING SPIES

1. Sarah Emma Edmonds, "Spies, Raiders & Partisans," The War for States' Rights, n.d., <http://civilwar.bluegrass.net/SpiesRaidersAndPartisans/sarahemmaedmonds.html> (June 12, 2003).

2. Mary Elizabeth Massey, *Bonnet Brigades* (New York: Alfred A. Knopf, 1966), p. 101.

3. Lerone Bennett, Jr., *Before the Mayflower: A History of Black America* (Chicago: Johnson Publishing Company, Inc., 1969), p. 146.

4. Agatha Young, *The Women and the Crisis* (New York: McDowell, Obolensky, 1959), p. 303.

5. Belle Boyd, *Belle Boyd in Camp and Prison* (London: Saunders, Otley, and Co., 1865), p. 106.

6. Massey, p. 87.

GLOSSARY

---

abolish—To end; to get rid of.

Amendment—A change made to the U.S. Constitution.

cavalry—Soldiers who fight on horseback.

civil war—A war between people of the same country.

Confederate States of America—The new nation formed by eleven Southern states that seceded from the United States of America: South Carolina, Mississippi, Florida, Alabama, Georgia, Louisiana, Texas, Virginia, Arkansas, North Carolina, and Tennessee. Also called the Confederacy.

emancipation—Setting someone free.

hoop skirt—A woman's skirt with a large, flexible circle placed at the bottom to make it puff out.

infantry—Soldiers who are trained to fight on foot.

plantation—A large farm.

quinine—A bitter substance that comes from the bark of the cinchona tree and is used in medicine.

secede—To withdraw from a group.

surgeon—A doctor who performs operations.

Underground Railroad—A secret network of escape routes and people who helped slaves run away to freedom.

Union—The Northern states that remained under the U.S. government during the Civil War.

FURTHER READING

Books

Caravantes, Peggy. *Petticoat Spies: Six Women Spies of the Civil War.* Greensboro, N.C.: Morgan Reynolds Publishers, 2002.

Chang, Ina. *A Separate Battle: Women and the Civil War.* New York: Puffin, 1996.

Raatma, Lucia. *Great Women of the Civil War.* Mankato, Minn.: Compass Point Books, 2005.

Sakany, Lois. *Women Civil War Spies of the Union.* New York: Rosen Publishing Group, 2004.

Silvey, Anita. *I'll Pass for Your Comrade: Women Soldiers in the Civil War.* New York: Clarion Books, 2008.

Internet Addresses

History.com: Women in the Civil War

<http://www.history.com/topics/women-in-the-civil-war>

National Archives: Women Soldiers of the Civil War

<http://www.archives.gov/publications/prologue/1993/spring/women-in-the-civil-war-1.html>

INDEX